COLCURFUL CHARACTERS
OF THE
ISLE OF WIGHT

by

C. W. R. WINTER

COACH HOUSE PUBLICATIONS LTD

ISBN No. 1-899-392-084

Published by
Coach House Publications Ltd
The Coach House, School Green Road, Freshwater,
Isle of Wight, PO40 9EB

Printed by
West Island Printers Ltd, Afton Road, Freshwater,
Isle of Wight, PO40 9TT

INTRODUCTION

The Isle of Wight's long and colourful history has produced a large number of outstanding personalities, people who through sheer force of character have left their mark on the Island and are remembered for their deeds, or misdeeds. A possibly greater number still have left no record behind them, perhaps through not being in the public eye. Even in our own day we have all met characters who are worthy of remembrance, but who are destined to remain unsung.

Of those who have managed to scrape into the history books, the following few are a representative sample. Would there were space for many more.

CONTENTS

White marble statue of Sir Robert in Yarmouth Church.

SIR ROBERT HOLMES

"... a man of understanding fitt to make a warr, and a courage to make it good; in the latter few goe beyond him; in the former few come short."

Sir William Coventry 1664

ONE of the most celebrated "overners" to live in the Island was Admiral Sir Robert Holmes, the rumbustious Governor of the Isle of Wight from 1668 to 1692, who lived in Yarmouth. Holmes was born in Ireland of English parents in about the year 1622, and he led an exciting and romantic life at a time when England was passing through a turbulent period of its history. Little is known of his early years, but he first came to notice as a young officer fighting for his King in the Civil War. Here he displayed conspicuous bravery and once saved the life of his commanding officer, who wrote of him in 1643:

"In the nick of time came up Mr Holmes to my assistance (who never failed me in time of danger)."

In 1646 after the battle of Oxford, which the Royalists lost, Prince Rupert (nephew of Charles I and General of the Royal forces) and his brother Maurice were permitted by Parliament to leave England for the continent, and Holmes went with them. He had achieved the rank of Major, though still only 24, but this was as high as he was to climb in the army, for he now found himself cast in the rôle of a sailor. In 1648 part of the English fleet defected and sailed for Holland and in due course it was fighting for the Royalists with Prince Rupert as its commander-in-chief.

During the next five years Holmes saw plenty of action at sea in a fleet which, though rapidly dwindling in size, carried on energetic piratical activities on behalf of the Royalist cause. The end came in 1653 when, with only one ship left, Prince Rupert left Holmes in charge in a French port to wind up the expedition.

No more was heard of Robert Holmes now until the restoration of the monarchy in 1660, but he was then soon in the news again, and by the autumn of that year was put in charge of a squadron of ships bound for West Africa on a mission which included trading, gold prospecting, and possibly a little trafficking in slaves. This mission was ostensibly peaceable, but as the Dutch were already established on the Guinea Coast, trouble was almost certain to ensue.

When he arrived off the Gambia an incident occurred which demonstrated very clearly the character of Holmes, and the fact that besides being a fearless and courageous leader who led from the front, he was also interested in the welfare of his men. He made arrangements to visit the King of Barra, 10 miles inland, and the King sent him a horse, since travelling on foot in the intense heat of the equator was difficult and dangerous. Holmes took with him a party of 25 men, including the captain of one of his ships, a Captain Stokes, and as Stokes was older and less fit than he, he gave Stokes the horse while he himself walked. Before leaving he gave orders that no guns were to be fired unless they wished to recall him urgently.

The march inland was exceedingly difficult, so much so that one man and a dog died on the way, and several others were distressed. The party arrived exhausted, and Holmes had only been with the King for 15 minutes when he heard guns firing. Assuming this was the urgent recall signal he immediately set off back to the coast, several of his men fainting on the way. Stokes stayed with the King, waiting for the cool of the evening.

When Holmes got back he discovered that it was Captain Stokes' ship that had fired – they were testing a new gun barrel – and apparently Stokes had never passed on the order not to fire except in an emergency. Holmes was naturally furious, and wrote in his diary:

> "Now I did heartily repent me of letting Stokes have the horse for I was so angry with him that I would have been well contented to have seen him hanged. I was three to four days so dazed in my head that I thought I should never have recovered."

From a Government point of view this expedition to the Gold Coast seems to have been a financial failure, though Holmes did bring back some gold. This was minted into coins which were subsequently christened "guineas". But Holmes himself returned a very wealthy man, and from this time onwards his lifestyle changed and verged on the magnificent.

If it is true that Holmes was the only one to profit from this venture, then it may be that his growing inability to get on with those above him, and the mistrust that he undoubtedly engendered, stems from this point. The Dutch Government protested bitterly at the high-handed way in which he had taken over their trading posts in Guinea, and though the English Government ignored this protest, and indeed sent him out again in 1663 on a similar mission which this time led to war – he was always subsequently regarded slightly with suspicion.

His relationship with Charles II, and his brother the Duke of York, can only be described as a "love-hate" one. The King later stayed with Holmes in Yarmouth on three occasions, and they were obviously men of similar tastes – Charles was notorious for the number of his mistresses and Holmes was a ladies' man too – but their friendship was interspersed with quarrels.

On his return from the first Guinea expedition Holmes was appointed Captain of the *Royal Charles*, the ship that had brought the King to England from exile, and had been chosen to fetch Catherine of Braganza from Lisbon, but his appointment did not last long. On sailing down the Thames he met a ship bringing the Swedish Ambassador to London, and failed to make her strike her sails, as was by protocol demanded. For this omission he was dismissed his ship by the King, who threatened him with further punishment.

He was soon given another command, though this caused him to quarrel with Samuel Pepys, Secretary of the Navy. Pepys had appointed a relative of his to the position of navigator and pilot on Holmes' ship and the latter refused to accept him, claiming that he was a drunkard and incompetent. Pepys was very worried about this quarrel, fearing that a duel might result, and was also concerned about the attentions Holmes was paying to Mrs Pepys. The quarrel was patched up but the two men were never friendly, and there is little doubt that Pepys was not only able to affect Holmes' career in the navy, but did so.

The second expedition to the Guinea Coast resulted in Holmes returning loaded with treasure, much of which it would appear he managed to keep for his own use. The Dutch again complained, and in order to appease them Holmes was committed to the Tower, where apparently he lived for a time in considerable comfort. When the Dutch ultimately declared war on England, Holmes was pardoned and released and was soon at sea again.

After the battle of Lowestoft (1665) in which Holmes distinguished himself, he fell out with the Duke of York, his Commander-in-Chief, who promoted another man over his head. In a fit of temper he offered to resign his Commission, and to his intense dismay the Duke accepted it. This was not the first time the two men had disagreed, and the Duke had possibly grown tired of trying to control Holmes, who was notoriously difficult to handle.

It was at this point that Holmes retired to the Isle of Wight. A few years previously he had been made Captain and Commander of Sandown Castle, a not very onerous appointment, but one that gave him a foothold in the Island, and he now retreated thither in bitterness, nursing his grievance against the Duke of York. He was appointed Deputy Governor of the Island and Captain of an Independent Company of Foot, and from then on until his death in 1692 he became increasingly involved in Island affairs, electing to live in Yarmouth where he could be close to the sea.

Later, in 1665, Charles II visited the Isle of Wight but refused to see Holmes as he had not patched up his quarrel with the Duke of York, but within a few months all was obviously forgiven as Holmes was called back to sea in command of a new ship, *The Defiance*, and was knighted by the King. Perhaps this was intended to be his last chance. In this ship he fought with great distinction in two battles against the Dutch, and was promoted to the rank of "Rear Admiral of the Red". He was still dissatisfied with this promotion, however, and felt he should have been advanced even further.

His greatest exploit in *The Defiance* was to lead a commando-type raid on the Dutch islands of Vlie and Schelling where there were many warehouses and a harbour for the large fleet of Dutch East Indiamen. His instructions were to carry out a swift raid lasting for a few hours, but in the event he found so many ships there that he (typically) took matters into his own hands and stayed considerably longer, burning in all about 150 ships and doing a considerable amount of damage. His own losses amounted to twelve men killed or wounded.

This was a remarkable achievement, particularly as his health, which had been failing for some time, was not good. When news of his success reached England the exploit was christened "Holmes' Bonfire" and church bells were rung in celebration throughout the land.

In January 1668 he was involved as a second to the Duke of Buckingham in his duel with the Earl of Shrewsbury, in which the latter and his second were both killed. As a result of this Holmes was convicted of murder, but was later reprieved.

In the same year he purchased the Governorship of the Isle of Wight from Lord Colepepper and energetically set about repairing the defences of the Island. He also acquired the titles of Vice-Admiral of the Isle of Wight, Governor and Vice-Admiral of Newport and Vice-Admiral of Hampshire, and was granted by the Crown two-thirds the value of any ship and goods, enemy or pretended neutral, taken on the high seas or in the ports, havens and creeks of his Vice-Admiralty. Under the terms of this agreement, which Holmes interpreted very freely, he conducted from his base in Yarmouth an operation which can only be described as piracy, but which added substantially to his already considerable wealth.

This halcyon state of affairs lasted for the next ten years, during which time the arthritis and gout from which he suffered grew steadily worse. His health did not prevent him, however, from fathering an illegitimate daughter, Mary, who was born in 1678 and who ultimately inherited his vast fortune. Little is known about her mother, nor for that matter about a possible marriage that he is said to have contracted c.1660. This was to a Christine Dalrymple, and all that is known about her is that she was an Edinburgh girl who travelled down by coach for the wedding, and suffered agonies of toothache on the way.

Holmes' last few years were far from peaceful and happy. Though increasingly infirm he survived the rebellion of 1688, staying loyal to the end to his old enemy the Duke of York, who as James II ultimately fled to the continent. In July 1689 Holmes was given permission to go to Bath to recruit his health.

> "I am now soe ill of my limbs that I have not been out of my chamber these twelve daies. I want the Bath as an old horse does Grass."

In 1690 he made almost his last public appearance when he sailed from Yarmouth up the Solent to Spithead to attend on the Queen of Spain who was visiting this country, but gout in his feet became so bad on this short voyage that when he arrived he could not climb aboard her ship.

He died in 1692 wracked with pain and worn out. He had lived a man's life, and had served his country faithfully and well, his only weakness being an inability to get on with those in authority over him. He was a born leader and his end was sad. But he left us a striking memorial to remember him by.

During his days as Governor of the Isle of Wight he captured a French ship carrying a white marble statue of Louis XIV, and also the sculptor, who was travelling to France to sculpt the head of the monarch from life. Sir Robert Holmes confiscated the statue, caused the sculptor to add the Holmes head, and directed that when he died this statue should be erected over his tomb.

For nearly 300 years now the statue has stood in Yarmouth church, a belligerent look on its face, a perpetual reminder of a great but human man. While it is there we shall not forget him.

St Helens Parish Church, where the Rev Mr Sidebotham officiated.

MRS SIDEBOTHAM

PERHAPS one of the most extraordinary characters ever seen in the Isle of Wight was the late Mrs Sidebotham (pronounced Sid-ee-both-am), wife of the Vicar of St Helens, and her story is given below. It is reprinted from a delightful little book entitled "Twelve Hundred Years in St Helens" by David Low and Sheila White, and I am most grateful for their kind permission to print it here.

"With the arrival of the Reverend Albert Ernest Sidebotham in May 1935 the village was about to be jolted out of its usual calm: not by Mr Sidebotham himself – he was a quiet, scholarly man, very well-read – but by his wife. At first, no-one knew about his wife or that he was even married. He arrived alone at the vicarage, having come from Portsmouth, where he had had an exhausting spell as Vicar of St George's, Portsea. This church is situated in the dockyard area, a tough locality, and because of this his health had deteriorated some-what. After he had been settled in for a few weeks, he announced one day that his wife would now be joining him: and she duly arrived.

When speaking – or writing – about Mrs Sidebotham it is diffi-cult to think of her as a single entity because she was never alone. With her – wherever she went – went her mother, her brother, her uniformed and cockaded chauffeur and her enormous car with crests on every door. The very first thing she told everyone who was introduced to her was that she had only married Mr Sidebotham on condition that he would allow her to have her first husband's photo-graph in every room of the house. It was difficult indeed to imagine – almost impossible – that two such entirely different people could possibly have ever, for a single moment, been attracted to each other – let alone get married.

Mr Sidebotham was a very shy man with, at times, a slight stutter or hesitation in his speech. As mentioned earlier, he was extremely well-read, a scholar, a clever and quiet man who loved to be alone with his books and surrounded by the lovely antique furni-ture that he collected. Mrs Sidebotham, on the other hand, was in appearance identical to the famous motion picture star, Mae West. She was frequently, when in London, asked for her autograph by people believing her to be the actress herself. Anyone who has seen

Mae West in photographs or films will not need to be told what she looked like – tall and very striking with an hour-glass figure. Mrs Sidebotham had all this and a flawless complexion, perfect teeth, and beautifully-done platinum blonde hair. She wore always ground-length dresses that clung to her figure and which were made of silver lamé, or black velvet, or rich brocades, or satins (sometimes they had small trains) cut very low; and she added deep necklaces of diamonds or pearls, and was swathed in white Arctic fox or luxurious sables. She always chose enormous, wide-brimmed hats, worn slightly to one side. Such style was something quite new in the village's experience, and – embarrassingly – St Helens church was packed to capacity every Sunday when the Vicar's wife was in residence.

The procession into Church was certainly imposing. Mrs Sidebotham would lead the way, sweeping-in – a vision of rich materials and flashing jewels, swirling furs and expensive perfume. Behind her came her brother, a dapper little man with a grey moustache, immaculately dressed in a light grey suit. He would be carrying rugs, hot-water bottles and prayer-books: these he would arrange under and around his sister in the front pew. Last came their mother; a little old lady attired in lamé and wearing a toque such as Queen Mary always wore, with an osprey standing up like a small fir tree on one side. Outside, the great crested car with its chauffeur waited.

Mrs Sidebotham never took any part in village activities, or visited, or did any of the things that a vicar's wife of those days was expected to do. The only times she ever appeared outside the vicarage was when she went to Church and when she condescended to distribute the prizes at the village sports. Then, resplendent and dazzling, she stood on a mat (laid down by her brother) on the Green and handed out prizes to small boys and girls too over-awed even to say "thank-you" for them. She was considered delicate and Mr Sidebotham would read out bulletins of his wife's health from time to time from the pulpit.

It was a very, very strange household and no-one was really surprised when one day before the war Mrs Sidebotham drove off in her car and she and her "entourage" were never seen again. Mr Sidebotham remained at St Helens for nearly twenty years, alone in the vicarage with his housekeeper and some cats. At the end of the war his wife was killed in a strange accident at Tangmere aerodrome in Sussex. The village was told by Mr Sidebotham that his wife had been doing some W.V.S. work and had driven in her car to Tangmere: there a Spitfire pilot had mistaken the landing strip and had crashed into her. Mr Sidebotham went to her funeral – the first time that he had been off the Island in three years. He then returned once more to his solitary life at St Helens, walking for miles around the parish, visiting. This must have been a great effort as he was lame by now and always used a stick.

Mr Sidebotham's health began to deteriorate in March 1952, and he was out of action for five months, until August of that year, and again for two months early in 1953. On February 28th 1954, he faltered when signing the register after the 8 a.m. service and did not officiate again. His funeral took place on March 27th in the same year and was conducted by the Bishop of Portsmouth. He was laid to rest in the Churchyard close by the entrance to the new section. He was much liked and it was sad that his home life did not appear to have been a happy one."

The late Sheila White, who wrote the above delightful little pen-portrait of Mrs Sidebotham, knew her personally. The first time they met was when the lady, with her customary bodyguard, visited her home to make a formal call. Unfortunately, as it was very hot, Sheila had decided to have a bathe in the sea, right opposite her house which is on the front at St Helens. She saw Mrs Sidebotham arrive, but feeling it would not be quite the thing to appear in her wet bathing costume, decided to stay in the water in the hope that once the good lady found she was out, the call would be a short one. Ultimately, however, she had to give in and return home, and of course, as she arrived at the door, dripping wet and with her hair all bedraggled, she ran slap into Mrs Sidebotham who had been waiting but had finally decided to leave. Life can have its very embarrassing moments.

John Nash, a most extraordinary man.

JOHN NASH

T HAT John Nash was a great architect there is no doubt, and that he also had a genius for town planning is equally well known, but what is perhaps not so often noted is that he was also a bit of a rascal. He was an opportunist and a very shrewd businessman, and after one false start his career zoomed as if jet propelled.

John Nash was born in 1752 in London, the son of an engineer and millwright. When he left school he became a pupil of Sir Robert Taylor, an architect who specialised in Palladian designs, and who held the Appointment of Architect to the Bank of England from 1765 to 1788. Under Taylor's guidance it was inevitable that Nash's own style should develop along the same lines.

When he was twenty-six John Nash inherited a little money and left Sir Robert Taylor's employ to set up on his own account as a speculative builder. But this venture did not succeed, and he quickly became bankrupt, which caused him to leave London and emigrate to Wales where he was soon practicing as an architect in Carmarthen. This time he was successful and slowly but steadily built up a practice in Wales and the West Country, two of his designs being for gaols in Carmarthen and Hereford.

His breakthrough came in 1796 when he was 44 years old. Back in London he had the good fortune to meet the Prince of Wales, who was later to become the The Prince Regent, and still later George IV. He became the Prince's personal architect, and from then on could do no wrong, though the success that this appointment brought him was not entirely due to his work. His friendship with the Prince of Wales led him, in 1798, to marry Mary Ann Bradley, a girl of 25, who was the Prince's mistress, and it has been suggested that this was a marriage of convenience, and that John Nash was a husband in name only. But Miss Bradley was about to have a baby, and it was necessary to give the child a name.

At this time John Nash suddenly became extremely rich, though since 1796 his life style had been reasonably affluent and he had been living in a smart town house he had re-built in Dover Street. But in 1798 the money began to flow in earnest. He bought land in East Cowes and started to build East Cowes Castle. This became his principal home, and right up until his death in 1835 he was continually altering and adding to it. In 1806 he bought more land and property at Hamstead and Ningwood in the West Wight, and at

Hamstead he re-built an old house for use as a shooting box. His architectural career in London also burgeoned to an astonishing degree, his output and achievement during the next 25 years being immense.

The patronage of the Prince of Wales provided him with opportunities out of the ordinary, and he seized them with both hands. John Nash has been criticized for the quality of his building work, but no-one can have anything but the greatest admiration for the diversity and sheer quantity of the buildings he designed, and for his incredible skill as a town planner. No architect, other than Sir Christopher Wren, has made such an impact on the design and layout of central London, and for this, if for nothing else, he will be remembered.

The list of his London planning projects and the buildings he designed goes on and on and on, and includes All Souls' Church, Langham Place, Bloomsbury Square, Carlton House Terrace, Clarence House, the Haymarket Theatre, Buckingham Palace, Marble Arch, the Royal Lodge, Windsor, and Regent Street. He was responsible for planning the whole of the Regent Street area, bringing order to the medieval chaos that existed at the time, and this project alone would have been sufficient to ensure him immortality, but he also created Regent's Park, the Regent's Canal, Waterloo Place, Trafalgar Square, and St James' Park. Outside London he designed such buildings as the Royal Stand at Ascot, and perhaps the most extraordinary one of all, the Royal Pavilion in Brighton. A breathtaking list.

In the Isle of Wight he was equally active, and designed the Guildhall in Newport and the building that is now the County Club in St James' Square. He designed and built St James' Church in East Cowes, St Mary's in West Cowes, and also Whippingham Church. The latter did not survive for long and was demolished by the Prince Consort who erected the present building. The body of the East Cowes Church also had to be re-built, and his own two houses, East Cowes Castle and Hamstead, ultimately had to be pulled down. Perhaps one of the problems was his devotion to stucco, which he exploited extensively, and which a wit at the time summed up in the following verse:

> "Augustus at Rome was for building renown'd,
> For of marble he left what of brick he had found;
> But is not our Nash, too, a very great master?
> He finds us all brick and he leaves us all plaster."

One of John Nash's friends in the Isle of Wight was Sir William Oglander of Nunwell, who had a passion for fresh air and hygiene. Nash executed a successful commission for him in re-building the stables and coach house at Nunwell, and then, realising that his client had a weak spot, persuaded him that oak panelling was unhygienic. Nunwell House was full of the most beautiful oak panelling at this time, and for the sum of £3,000 Nash ripped it all out and replaced it with wallpaper. No doubt he then sold the panelling to someone else. Sir William was perfectly happy with the transaction, so John Nash then produced plans for the complete demolition of Nunwell House and its replacement with a Palladian design of mansion. But here Lady Oglander interposed and put her foot down very firmly, banning any future alterations or desecrations. In defence of John Nash it must be said that old oak panelling frequently harboured rats, and from this point of view wallpaper probably was more hygienic.

On the subject of Nash's private life there has been much conjecture. In a fascinating biography by Terence Davis, the author says that Mrs Nash had five children in all, the first, Thomas, being born at the time of her marriage. The others, who came along at intervals, were Anne, James, Sarah and John, and all of them were called Pennethorne. The Nashes entertained lavishly at East Cowes Castle, but after John Nash's death his widow retired to the Hamstead house with Anne, Sarah, and later John. Terence Davis says she lived in considerable style, surrounded by Royal relics, until her death in 1851. He also says:

> "After her death the money to keep up the house suddenly dropped, although the Pennethorne family continued to live there on a reduced scale until 1923. The possibility that the children were royal bastards has been denied and confirmed by successive generations of their descendants, largely depending on their attitude to illegitimacy, royal or otherwise."

Thomas, a gifted painter, died young. Anne was living at Hamstead at the time of her mother's death, and Sarah and John also lived there. James became an architect, and chief assistant to Nash, and was knighted in 1870. John also became an architect, and produced a book on architecture in 1878. Hamstead passed out of the Pennethorne possession in the early 1920s and a discreet veil has been drawn over their subsequent history. Rumours have inevitably circulated, perhaps the most intriguing ones being that Queen Victoria herself felt uneasy about them, and that they were provided with a private income for life on condition that they remained unmarried and childless.

But what sort of a man was John Nash? His one time partner, George Repton, went on record to say that he was upset at not being given credit for any of the designs he originated, Nash publishing them under his own name, and he wrote:

". . . amongst the melancholy evils to which human life is subject, the most excruciating to a man of sensibility is the remembrance of disappointed hope from misplaced confidence."

A Mrs Arbuthnot said:

"Mr Nash is a very clever, odd, amusing man, with a face like a monkey's, but civil and good-humoured to the greatest degree."

In another excellent biography, entitled "The Life and Work of John Nash, Architect" by Sir John Summerson, Nash's style is described as follows:

"There is no studied medievalism in any of Nash's works; his "Gothic" vocabulary was so limited that to call it rudimentary would be an overstatement. Nor did he attempt to elaborate any system of ornament appropriate to the Italian vernacular mood. The effect of his great houses is one of picturesque 'movement' with a rather off-hand stylistic characterisation in the direction of Gothic, Tudor, or Italian, or indeed a combination of any two – or three."

When John Nash died, *The Annual Register* dismissed him with the following obituary:

"As a speculative builder, this gentleman amassed a large fortune; but as an architect he did not achieve anything that will confer on him lasting reputation."

But another obituary, by Theodore Hook, Editor of *John Bull*, and incidentally brother of the Rector of Whippingham, paints a very different picture:

"Let the reader recollect the huddled mass of wretched streets and houses which 20 years ago covered the site of Regent Street, the Quadrant, and Waterloo Place; let the reader recollect the still more wretched courts and alleys, dens of infamy and haunts of thieves, which maze-like spread themselves from St Martin's Church to the neighbourhood of Covent

Garden; let him now look upon the range of buildings and the handsome streets which occupy their places . . . Let the reader, we say, turn his eyes to that magnificent adjunct of London, the Regent's Park, now one of the healthiest and gayest of the public walks and drives, a creation of the mind of Mr Nash.

In private life Nash was a warm and sincere friend, his mind, active and comprehensive as it was, was singularly natural and simple; his conception was quick and clear; his thoughts were original, and his conversation was both instructive and pre-eminently agreeable. He was, in fact, a most extraordinary man."

Prince Charles, later King Charles II, who befriended Sir Henry.

SIR HENRY MAINWARING

STRICTLY speaking, Sir Henry Mainwaring was not an Islander, although he knew the Island well and visited it on many occasions. But he was fairly closely related to Sir John Oglander, being a cousin of Lady Oglander's, and perhaps this is sufficient qualification for him to be included under this heading, for his character and his career were both colourful in the extreme and well worth recounting.

The following description of him was written by Mr W. H. Long, who in 1888 published "The Oglander Memoirs", being extracts from Sir John Oglander's diaries. Sir Henry Mainwaring is of course mentioned in the Memoirs, and Mr Long was so intrigued with him that he carried out considerable further research, and then wrote the following account:

"Captain (afterwards Sir Henry) Mainwaring was the son of Sir George Mainwaring, Kt, of Ighfield, Shropshire, by Anne, daughter of Sir William More, of Moseley, Surrey. In 1611 he was appointed Captain of St Andrew's Castle, Hants; but soon growing dissatisfied with his lot, and longing for a more adventurous life, he threw up his command and put to sea in the bark *Nightingale*, with the license of the Lord Admiral, under the pretext of making a voyage to Guiana. His first intention was to plunder the Spaniards beyond the line, but he no sooner reached the Straits of Gibraltar, than he gave full vent to his predatory inclinations. Lying off Cape Spartel he captured every Spanish vessel he could master, with now and then a Frenchman or Dunkirker; but he always respected the flag of his country. He overhauled a bark from Lubeck entering a Spanish port and, after rifling the cargo, dismissed the crew in peace. A Galway merchant on board claimed the cargo as his, and in proof of his assertion pointed out that the goods were consigned to an English factor for sale. Mainwaring anchored off the port, sent for the factor to come on board, and finding the statement of the merchant true, restored at once the whole of his plunder. When unable to keep the sea, or in need of a refit, he was always sure of a welcome with his prizes in the ports of the Emperor of Morocco. In 1616 he was in the Channel, and at Dover agreed to purchase a ship with her ordnance, belonging to Joachim Wardeman, of Lubeck, for £200; but not being used to this slow way of dealing, or perhaps not having the money, he seized the ship without payment. Wardeman complained to the King, who ordered the ship to be restored; and Mainwaring's crew being 'stayed' when on shore, he found his occupation, if not gone, growing exceedingly perilous, so he sought for and purchased a pardon, which was granted him in 1617.

Mainwaring rapidly rose in favour; he was knighted in March 1618, and in 1620 was appointed Lieutenant of Dover Castle by Lord Zouch, Warden of the Cinque Ports, by whose order his crew had been 'stayed' a few years before. Some time after, on receiving the Spanish Ambassador at Dover, he was pleasantly told by that dignitary 'that he would excuse him 12 crowns out of the millions he owed the Spaniards, if he would pay the rest'. Though holding a responsible post under the Government, he did not adapt his manners to his station, but still acted like an improvident roystering buccaneer; always ready for a carouse or brawl, not over scrupulous in his transactions, and preferring to hear the chimes at midnight anywhere but within the walls of Dover Castle.

This could not last, complaints arose, and in March 1621 Lord Zouch wrote to him from Bramshill, that in consequence of his conduct in frequent absences from the Castle, at Canterbury, and elsewhere, sleeping in the town at night, brawling and fighting in the street, and disorderly life generally, he requested him to resign his appointment. He proceeded to say that he wished to part fairly and quietly with him, but if he made any objection, he should be obliged to take some other course. Sir Henry attempted to defend his conduct, and tried hard to keep his place, the loss of which, he said, 'would be ten times worse than if he had never enjoyed it'.

Finding that the Warden was determined to be rid of him, he applied to Secretary Conway for a Captain's place in a King's ship; which resulted in the Secretary writing to Lord Zouch, requesting that Mainwaring might go as Captain with the Earl of Rutland in the ship which was about sailing for Spain to bring home Prince Charles and the Infants, with the chance of resuming his office on his return. The Warden replied that he would have rejoiced at the preferment of his Lieutenant, but for his displeasure at his cunning practices, that he had already sent him a friendly dismissal, and that he only held his place on condition of surrendering it when required to do so. But rather than Mainwaring should be placed as a curb upon him, he would resign his own office, and retire into private life himself.

Sir Henry received his appointment as Captain under the Earl of Rutland in the *Prince Royal*, which ship, with others for the voyage to Spain, being fitting out at Portsmouth, he proceeded thither, and in the absence of the Earl acted as superintendent of the fleet. All possible expedition was required, and the Superintendent was equal to the demands of the occasion. In a letter to Rutland he says he had got things in strict order, had put his coxswain in the bilboes for being drunk; and a man who stole a jerkin was, by his command, ducked at the yard arm, and then towed ashore at the stern of a boat and dismissed. In August 1623, while the ships were lying at Portsmouth, James I, who had been staying at Beaulieu in the New Forest for some days, paid an unexpected visit to the fleet, and dined on board the *Prince Royal*, where in the absence of the Earl of Rutland, Sir Henry probably received the King.

On the return voyage from Spain, he succeeded in gaining the favourable notice of Prince Charles who, shortly after his return in November 1623, wrote to Lord Zouch, requesting him to reinstate Mainwaring as his Lieutenant at Dover. Zouch, in his reply to Secretary Nicholas, stated that rather than restore the place to Mainwaring, he would go to execution, or submit to any punishment. Mainwaring succeeded in persuading the Prince that he had been badly treated and wronged by Lord Zouch, but Lord Carlisle said it was injurious to believe the assertions of such a man against 'an ancient baron, grave counsellor, and religious, well-deserving gentleman'. By the direction of the Warden, a paper containing the reasons for the dismissal of Sir Henry was presented to the Council, with a statement signed by the Clerk of Dover Castle, the Sergeant of the Admiralty Records there, and others, declaring that during Mainwaring's lieutenancy, he was often absent from the Castle, so that Warrants could not be signed, nor oaths administered; that to remedy this he would sign blank warrants, and leave them with the Clerk to fill up as he pleased; and that by running into debt and keeping low company, he degraded his office. That he had endeavoured to get possession of £8,000 or £9,000 which was in the charge of the Sergeant of the Admiralty, but not succeeding, he vainly persuaded the Sergeant to cheat the merchants who were the owners, by tearing the bags and mixing all the money together, so that none of the owners should know their own.

These representations settled the matter, Sir Henry was never replaced, and soon after Sir John Hippisley was appointed Lieutenant of Dover Castle. Exasperated by his dismissal and the loss of his emoluments, Mainwaring in March 1624 opposed the election of Zouch's nominees for Dover, Sir R. Young and Sir E. Cecil, and succeeded in depriving them of their seats, as not being elected according to law. In the same year Lord Zouch, being old and infirm, on consideration of £1,000 ready money and £500 per year for life, resigned his patent as Lord Warden of the Cinque Ports to the Lord Admiral Buckingham; with a special proviso that the Clerk of Dover Castle and the Sergeant of the Admiralty should retain their places; and that the Duke should not admit Sir H. Mainwaring to any office in the ports, on account of his labouring for the disgrace of Lord Zouch, both in Court and in Parliament, and threatening revenge on the poor men who testified to his misdemeanours.

This arrangement does not seem to have much affected his interest at Court, as in 1626 he was appointed one of the special Commissioners for enquiring into the state of the Navy; and in 1637 he was one of the Captains selected by the King for service under Sir John Pennington. He was an unsuccessful candidate for the Surveyorship of the Navy in 1619; but in the same year sailed as Vice-Admiral to Sir J. Pennington in the *Rainbow* for Scotland and took on board at Berwick and Newcastle a number of Scottish prisoners, whom he conveyed to London, but shortly after their arrival they were all set at liberty. In the Civil War Sir Henry supported the Royal cause, and was with Lord Hopton in Cornwall; and in 1647 he with other impecunious Cavaliers was at Jersey with young Prince Charles, afterwards Charles II. When the Prince left Jersey for France, Mainwaring still remained there, then being an old man between 70 and 80 years of age.

Here, in his leisure hours, he entertained the simple-minded chronicler of the Island, Jean Chevalier, with the most astounding recitals of his adventures and heroic feats in his freebooting days; how the Emperor of Morocco and himself were on such familiar terms that they always addressed each other as 'brother'; that on one occasion, being attacked by a superior force, after expending all his shot, he loaded his guns with pieces of eight and repulsed the enemy; and finally, that he rescued Charles I when Prince of Wales in Spain from the Spaniards, and at the same time beguiled several Spanish Grandees aboard his ship, and brought them captives to England, to his own and the King's advantage. Sir Henry in his old age must have been a garrulous and agreeable companion who knew well how to spin 'a sailor's yarn'.

After this we hear no more of him, and he probably died before the Restoration in 1660."

JAMES HARRINGTON

WHEN Charles I was originally imprisoned in Carisbrooke Castle towards the end of 1647 he was allowed a reasonable retinue of servants. All of these were picked for their loyalty to the King, and it was not long before a two-way communication system was set up and correspondence began to be exchanged between the King and his supporters outside. Once this was operational it became very much easier to co-ordinate an escape attempt. Parliament of course knew what was going on, for their Derby House Committee (an organisation consisting of seven members of the House of Lords and thirteen Commons) had its own network of anonymous agents whose job was to gather information. In February 1648 the Committee warned Colonel Hammond, Captain of Carisbrooke Castle and the King's gaoler, that an escape was being planned, and as a result of this the number of the King's servants was reduced, and some on whom suspicion rested were replaced.

Two new Grooms of the Bedchamber were appointed at this time, and one of these was a man called James Harrington. From a security point of view the Grooms were key men, for they had daily access to and close contact with the King, so that it was most important to the Parliamentary authorities that they should be trustworthy. James Harrington was born in 1611, the eldest son of Sir Sapcotes Harrington of Rutland. He was educated at Trinity College, Oxford, and after graduation had travelled extensively in Europe. Besides being well-read he was intelligent, had a sense of humour, was a good mixer in any society, and above all was regarded as being "safe".

But in this last requirement he turned out to be something of a disappointment to his Parliamentary employers. He got on well with the King, which was certainly to be desired, but the more they came into contact with each other, the closer they became, and the more Harrington sympathised with the King's predicament. As for the King, it was said that he loved Harrington's company, and chose rather to talk with him than with any other of his immediate staff. So it is not surprising to find that, after the failure of the March escape plan, the Derby House Committee were warning Colonel Hammond in April that another escape plot was hatching, and that they believed that Harrington had agreed to help the King.

King Charles I's prison in Carisbrooke Castle.

As all the world knows, this second escape attempt in May also failed, and that the King, following the abortive effort to negotiate an agreement with the Parliament – the so-called Treaty of Newport – was taken back to the mainland, was tried on a charge of treason and ultimately executed in January 1649. Through all this tragic period James Harrington remained loyal to the King, and indeed stayed with him to the very end on the scaffold in Whitehall.

After the King's death Harrington occupied himself in writing a book which he called "Oceana". This book was an allegory, describing what he considered would be an ideal Commonwealth, and putting forward the theory that power should come from the ownership of land, for only land is stable and permanent. He envisaged the growth of a middle-class, who would exercise the function of government, the principal feature of which would be the election of councillors and the rotational retirement of these. It could be said that James Harrington was a little ahead of his time.

The book came to the notice of Oliver Cromwell who was highly suspicious of it, and who seized the manuscript as it was being set up for printing. Harrington was very upset at this, and tried every way he could to recover the book, but to no avail. Finally, in desperation he decided to appeal to Lady Claypole, Cromwell's favourite daughter, whom he had heard was approachable and kind-hearted.

He called at Lady Claypole's house and was ushered into a room in which he found a small girl, three years old, playing by herself. The child was friendly, and very soon James Harrington was joining in her game. When her mother came into the room the child was in his arms at the window and he was pointing out something in the garden to her.

Harrington introduced himself to the lady and, putting the child down at her feet, told her she had entered just in time to prevent him stealing the charming little girl. The mother expressed surprise at this, for what could he possibly want with one so young, she was of far too tender years to be his mistress. Harrington replied gently that it was not love that would have prompted the theft, but revenge.

Lady Claypole again expressed surprise and asked what injury she had done him, to which he explained that it was not her but her father who was at fault, and that he wished to prevail upon her to intercede with her father to return the child that he had stolen from Harrington. It is impossible, said the lady, that my father would steal your child, he has plenty of children of his own, to which Harrington replied that it was the child of his brain that had been stolen, and he told her the story of "Oceana".

The way in which he had presented his case so impressed Lady Claypole that she agreed to do what she could, and indeed her intercession with her father was completely successful. Cromwell read the book, professed to like it, and agreed to its printing, whereat the author gratefully dedicated it to him.

After this successful outcome to his problems, and the public approval of the Lord Protector, James Harrington appeared to have no further worries, but Life has a nasty habit of dealing one a blow when it is least expected, and this now happened to him. At the Restoration in 1660 the book "Oceana" once more attracted unfavourable attention, and Harrington came under suspicion on account of the Republican ideas he had promulgated. In December 1661 he was sent to the Tower on a charge of "treasonable practices and designs", and though he made repeated pleas of innocence, and pointed to the loyalty with which he had served King Charles I, these all went unheeded.

Maybe he became an embarrassment to Authority, for suddenly without warning he was transferred to St Nicholas' Island, a barren and primitive rock situated in Plymouth Sound. This was such a shock to his system that his health was affected, and though, after repeated requests, he was moved back to the mainland at Plymouth, where conditions were slightly less rigorous, his mind became deranged.

The Governor of Plymouth interceded with the King, on his behalf, and ultimately the injustice of what had taken place was realised, and he was released and returned to London. In due course his physical health improved but alas he was a broken man, and never recovered his full mental powers. Though he lived on for a number of years, and even got married, the rest of his life was melancholy as he reflected bitterly on the folly of putting one's trust in Princes – or for that matter, in Parliaments.

SOPHIE DAWES

IN 1792 a daughter was born to a St Helens fisherman and his wife, the third of their three children. The father's name was Dawes, Dickie Dawes, well-known locally as a fisherman and a smuggler, and something of a character in his own right. As a smuggler he achieved fame throughout the Island for his exploits in outwitting the Excise Men, and for the boldness with which he landed his cargoes of brandy, silk and tobacco. His knowledge of local waters was unparalleled, and he found a passage through the rocks off Bembridge where the Customs men dared not follow him. This is still known today as Dickie Dawes' Gut. He was a rough, tough, extrovert character, more interested in his smuggling activities than in fishing, and not above sampling the brandy which he regularly brought back from France. His third child, Sophie, inherited many of his characteristics.

Dickie Dawes' wife, Jane, was a member of another well-known Island family of fishermen, the Calloways, and as soon as they were old enough the three children were involved in winkle gathering on the beach as a means of augmenting the family's income. With this background the odds were very heavily in favour of little Sophie Dawes growing up and ultimately marrying a fisherman before settling down to a humdrum conventional life in St Helens, bringing up her own family. No-one could possibly have forecast, not even with the wildest flights of imagination, the fantastic career that this little girl was to build for herself, a career that was to take her from the humble background of a fisherman's cottage to the highest levels of society, both in this country and in France.

When Sophie was ten years old her father died, leaving the family destitute and unable to fend for themselves, so the whole family was taken into the House of Industry in Parkhurst, where they were looked after and contributed to their keep by doing work provided for them. At thirteen Sophie was sent out to work for a local farmer, and she survived in his household for two years but then walked out on him and went to Portsmouth. Here she found herself a job as a chambermaid in an hotel but this did not satisfy her for long. She was growing up fast and already beginning to realise that life had more to offer than being a simple chambermaid. Though not a great beauty she was attractive and well developed, and obviously had what later became known as sex appeal.

Sophie Dawes' Cottage, her birthplace in St Helens.

This she took with her to London, and here her career really began to blossom. Her first job was as a milliner's assistant but she was soon fired from this on account of a love affair that interfered with the business of the shop. From the milliners she graduated to Covent Garden Theatre where for a time, like Nell Gwynn, she sold oranges, and it is believed she may even have appeared on the stage.

She was now mixing with men of a slightly higher social standing, and she enthusiastically seized the opportunity of exploiting her charms to the full. Before long she became the mistress of an army officer, who installed her in a smart villa in Turnham Green, and though this arrangement did not last she emerged from it with an annuity of £50 and a burning determination to use the experience as a stepping stone to something better. For a time she was employed on administrative duties in a high class Piccadilly brothel, and this produced the opportunity she had been awaiting.

Here she met a Frenchman who was servant to the exiled Duc de Bourbon, and who recommended her to his master. The Duke, aged 52 and one of the richest men in France, was living a rather frustrating life in exile, unable to reach his vast wealth in his own country, but still in possession of sufficient funds to live comfortably in London. He was delighted with Sophie, who was now flying very high indeed, and though there seems to be some confusion as to how she actually became his mistress, there is no doubt that at one point the Duc de Bourbon played a game of cards with the Duke of Kent, Queen Victoria's father, with Sophie as the prize, and as a result of this she passed from one man to the other.

The Duc de Bourbon certainly looked after Sophie Dawes extremely well, buying her a splendid house in Bloomsbury and settling on her £800 a year as pocket money. He lavished money, jewels and property on her, and perhaps the most extraordinary gift of all – he paid for her education. Equally extraordinary was the gratitude and avidity with which Sophie accepted this latter gift, and for three years she worked hard at learning French, Latin, Greek, music, singing and dancing. This says much for her intelligence and determination, and though she never lost the roughness of her naturally coarse nature, she at least acquired enough polish and veneer to enable her to be accepted in Society.

In 1814 the Restoration in France made it possible for the Duke to return to his native land and reclaim his estates. He tried desperately hard to leave Sophie behind, but she was determined not to lose him and followed him to Paris. The Duke's father died in 1818 and the Duke not only became very much richer but also succeeded to the title of Prince. Sophie was now even more determined to cling to him, and in the end he agreed that she should come to live in his Palace, and should be introduced to all and sundry as his illegitimate daughter.

To make the situation look thoroughly respectable a marriage was arranged for Sophie with a Monsieur de Fouchères, an officer in the French Guards who shortly afterwards was created a Baron, so that it could be said that Sophie Dawes, the fisherman's daughter from St Helens, had really arrived. Unfortunately she was not content to lead a conventional and respectable life, and as she got older the coarser side of her nature became predominant. As well as being the Prince's mistress she had innumerable affairs with a variety of unsuitable men, and became increasingly quarrelsome and domineering. She exercised a strange but powerful influence over everyone with whom she came in contact, and she was forever in the public eye as she floated around Paris escorted by a host of servants. Inevitably her husband found out the truth of her relationship with the Prince, and in order to preserve his honour he horsewhipped her. A divorce followed, and she received much adverse publicity.

As the Prince grew older and feebler their relationship soured, and he found himself increasingly unable to cope with her tantrums and bullying, and her desperate attempts to get her hands on a sizeable slice of his fortune. After continual badgering he made a Will by which she was to receive twelve million francs, but once he had done this she began to worry that he might change his mind, and she came to the conclusion that the sooner he died, the better.

The Prince was alarmed to find that her attitude towards him was becoming menacing, and he began to fear for his life. These fears unfortunately were well founded, and one morning his valet found him hanging in his room. It was supposed to look like suicide, but there were strong suspicions of foul play, so strong in fact that members of his family kicked up a fuss, and even contested the Will. France was thereupon entertained to a first-class and protracted scandal in the courts that implicated many people in high places, including the King himself. Sophie became an object of universal contempt, and in due course when the going got too hot she felt it prudent to leave France and return to England.

Once back in this country she bought an estate in Hampshire and a large house in the West End of London near Hyde Park, and here three years later she died. She had grown fat and coarse and was suffering from dropsy, but it was an unexpected heart attack that actually killed her. She gave away much money to charity before she died, but left a small fortune to her nephew William Henry Dawes, who re-built two manor houses in the Isle of Wight, at Wydcombe and Gotten, and also left his name on the Hoy Monument on St Catherine's Down.

So ended one of the most remarkable women the Isle of Wight has ever seen. She was not a very savoury character, and may even have been a murderess, but she was possessed of tremendous drive inherited from her father, and was by no means all bad. She looked after her mother, her elder sister, and other members of her family, and kept them in comfort all their lives, and any evil in her may have been a product of the society in which she lived. In a corrupt French Court she not only held her own, but was at home, giving as good as she got. For a girl of such humble origin her achievement was outstanding, and for this she will be remembered.

Memorial to Robert Hook in the road named after him, Hooke Hill, leading up to the Church.

ROBERT HOOKE

Hooke hill in Freshwater is named after Robert Hooke who was born on 18th July 1635, son of the Rector of Freshwater, whose church lay near the top of the hill. He was a small, weakly child, and for the first seven years of his life his health was so precarious that there were times when he was not expected to live. But what Robert Hooke lacked in physical strength was more than compensated by his extraordinary mental powers, for this puny child was possessed of a massive brain, which when he grew up ranked him with the foremost scientists and philosophers of the day. Even as a small boy he showed astonishing engineering ability, his hobby being the making of mechanical toys – including a fully rigged ship that fired guns as it sailed along.

Even when fully grown he was small in stature, thin and crooked, and is said to have had a mean and furious temper, together with sordid personal habits, which made him unpopular with his fellow men. But his brain was superhuman and a biographer has said of him:

> "He had a remarkable fertility and quickness of mechanical invention, his speculations reaching over the whole field of natural philosophy from the minutest disclosures of the microscope to beyond the furthest sweep of the telescope."

His father was able to give him a good education, sending him to Westminster School, and later to Christchurch, Oxford. At Oxford he became part of a small group of men who –

> "began to knock at the door at which truth was to be found, though it was left to Newton to force it open."

The group to which Hooke belonged included John Wilkins, afterwards Bishop of Chester (who married Robina, sister of Oliver Cromwell); John Wallis, theologian, scholar, logician and mathematician; Seth Ward, later Bishop of Exeter and then Salisbury, an astronomer; Francis Glisson, pioneer in medical research; Thomas Wallis, researcher on the brain and the nervous system; Christopher Wren, mathematician and astronomer before he became an architect; and the Hon. Robert Boyle, philosopher. The above is a formidable list of brains, and the unofficial "Club" that they formed in Oxford became later, in 1662, the Royal Society, with a Charter from the King, and Dr Hooke the first Secretary and Curator. Hooke assisted

Boyle in many of his chemical experiments, and is credited with having divined the theory of oxygen as the element in the atmosphere which sustains combustion and animal life.

In 1665, the year before the Great Fire, he published a book "Micrographia" which brought him scientific and literary acclaim, and after the fire he put forward a plan for the re-building of the City, as a result of which he was appointed City Surveyor, a position that made him a rich man. The Royal Society, under the patronage of Charles II, went on from strength to strength, and as well as being one of the oldest societies of its kind in Europe, rapidly established itself as one of the most important. Throughout its whole existence it has zealously and generously supported all types of scientific research, and is still held in great international esteem.

Hooke continued his own scientific work and carried out valuable research into the vibration of bodies, and he also put forward new geological theories. He disputed with Newton over the latter's theory of light, and claimed that he had anticipated many of the findings. It can truly be said of him that he advanced the frontiers of knowledge in many directions by his continual probing and questioning, and it has been claimed that he had the power of penetrating into the secrets of nature before the evidence was unfolded.

Later in life he was involved in a law suit which was resolved in his favour on his birthday, 18th July, and he is recorded as saying:

> "I was born on this day of July 1635, and God hath now given me a new birth. May I never forget His mercies to me; while He gives me breath may I praise Him!"

As he saw death approaching he became a "workaholic" and he died, worn out, on 3rd March 1702. The Island has produced many famous sons, but none more illustrious than Robert Hooke of Freshwater.

WILLIAM PORTER

WILLIAM PORTER was a Newport man who lived at the end of the 18th century. For many years he made a satisfactory living by baking meat pies and hawking them about the streets, and they were obviously of very good quality, for though he sold them for only one penny each, he prospered and was able to save a considerable sum of money. This enabled him to buy the house in which he lived, and once it was in his possession he set about re-building it.

This experience gave him a taste for building, and presumably he was able to sell his house at a profit, for he gave up baking and selling meat pies and decided to pursue a career as a builder. His next venture was a bold one, for he built a water mill, and a large one at that. This was on the east bank of the Medina River at the mouth of Claybrook Luck, and it was a tide mill. There is no doubt it was a very ambitious project for a beginner to tackle, but William Porter made a success of it.

An amusing story is told about the name of this mill. Officially it was called the East Medina Mill, but in 1790 at the time it was being built, convict ships were lying off the Mother Bank near Ryde, loading prisoners for the Botany Boy penal settlement in Australia. It happened that William Porter's workmen building the mill were taken down the river to the site by boat each morning, and wags on the quay at Newport suggested that really they were being taken to the convict ships bound for Botany Bay. In this way the mill became known as Botany Bay Mill, and when Porter built another mill on the west bank of the Medina this one was given the nickname of the Port Jackson (Sydney) Mill.

In between building these two mills William Porter built a row of seven elegant houses at the bottom end of Newport High Street, and these became known as Porter's Row. All seemed to be going well for the builder, and in 1793 he built a third tide mill, at Yarmouth. This building is now a private house, and stands picturesquely at the point where the Thorley Brook enters the estuary of the River Yar, just to the south of the town.

William Porter then announced that he would next be building a crescent of fine houses in Cowes, but Fate decreed otherwise, and as so often happens in Life it dealt him a sudden, swift blow that caused the little empire he was building to crash to the ground. As a

Yarmouth Mill, built by William Porter, baker of meat pies.

humble baker of meat pies he had never learned to read or write, and consequently had not been able to keep any accounts of his several building transactions, all the necessary paper work being done by the Newport Bank that organised the finance. This Bank now got into serious financial difficulties and closed its doors, leaving poor William Porter friendless and alone.

It transpired that he had made two serious mistakes. The first was that due to ignorance of business methods he had not secured his property on adequate leases, and though the two Medina Mills were sold for £9,000 it would seem that this money was absorbed in the Bank's deficiency, for William Porter got nothing for them. His second mistake was his extravagance in keeping three horse-drawn vehicles, a phæton and pair, a post chaise, and a single horse chaise, which were really beyond his means.

Sadly, all the buildings he erected, with one exception, have now disappeared – the exception being Yarmouth Mill, which remains as a memorial to this strange entrepreneur who built his business on insecure foundations, and who in the end was left penniless. We are not told why he did not return to baking meat pies, nor are we told why his friends in the Methodist Church, of which he was a staunch supporter, could not help him. All we know is that in 1794, in the prime of life, he died in poverty, an example to all of a man who had bitten off more than he could chew.

Yarmouth Town Hall, seat of the Town Council, who in 1721 "elected" Stanwix to represent them in Parliament.

GENERAL
THOMAS STANWIX

THE ancient Borough of Yarmouth was first invited to send a representative to Parliament in 1295, and this connection with central Government continued in an unbroken line for over 500 years until the passing of the Reform Bill in 1832, the only change during that time being that in 1584 representation was increased from one man to two. Many of those who represented Yarmouth at Westminster were not local men at all, and there were no elections, the representatives being appointed by the Town Council in return for a cash consideration, and indeed it was the increasing corruption of this practice that led ultimately to the Reform Bill.

In the Parliament of 1721 one of the Yarmouth members was General Thomas Stanwix, a distinguished soldier who had fought under Marlborough and who had had a career in the Marines. He came of an old Carlisle family, and at one time represented Carlisle in Parliament, after which he was successively Governor of Kingston-upon-Hull, Governor of Carlisle Castle, and Lieutenant Governor of the Isle of Wight. He died in 1776, and the following true story is told for the sake of its curiosity.

Thomas Stanwix lost his first wife in 1759 and married again in 1763. In 1776 he and his second wife, and his only daughter by his first wife, took ship in the *Eagle* from Canada to England but ran into bad weather in the North Atlantic, which resulted in the ship foundering. There were no survivors.

By the marriage settlement on his second marriage his personal property was to go in one direction if he survived his wife, in another direction if his wife survived him, and in a third if his daughter survived them both. As there were no witnesses to the calamity that had caused the death of all three of them, a Suit in Chancery was instituted to decide in what order they had died.

One Counsel maintained that the two ladies would have been down below and would therefore have died sooner than the General who would have been on deck, and by swimming or clinging to the rigging would have survived longer.

The second Counsel said that on the contrary the General would have exerted himself to put his wife in as much safety as possible, and thus she would have survived him and her step-daughter, who would have had to fend for herself.

The third Counsel could not agree with either of the above hypotheses, and maintained that the girl, being younger and more active, would have survived her parents, whereas they would probably have rushed into each others arms and thus unwittingly have frustrated their individual efforts to escape.

The case lasted for a year, providing employment for a number of well qualified and highly paid lawyers, without reaching a definite conclusion, and in the end the Court emulated the Judgement of Solomon by recommending that they should split the money three ways.

One barrister, a Mr Ferne, intrigued by the niceties of the situation, left among his papers two most ingenious arguments – one proving that the General survived his daughter, and the other that his daughter survived him. Both are said to be equally conclusive, but they were never published as Mr Ferne felt it was immoral for a barrister to argue first on one side and then on the other in the same case. He wrote these proofs purely for his own amusement and it was not until after his death that they came to light.

JOHN, LORD CUTTS

LORD CUTTS came to the Isle of Wight as Governor in 1692 on the death of Sir Robert Holmes, and retained that position until his own death in 1707, although he actually spent very little time in the Island. Cutts was a man of culture, educated in Cambridge, but a complex character with an imperious nature whose greatest attribute was personal bravery. In 1685 he published a book of poems which was well received, his verse being described as graceful and delicate.

But only a year later Addison, in a Latin poem, was extolling Cutts' bravery at the siege of Breda, and there is no doubt that he was never happier than when he was fighting. In 1689 he again distinguished himself at the Battle of the Boyne, and was awarded an Irish peerage. He was present at the capture of Namur in 1695, a battle that has been described as the greatest military exploit which England had achieved in Europe since the days of Crecy, Poitiers, and Agincourt. At Namur Cutts played a gallant part in coolly rallying the English troops when the battle was hottest. Macaulay commented that his bravery was conspicuous, and said:

> "In that bull-dog courage which flinches from no danger however terrible, he was unrivalled. He was so much at his ease in the hottest fire of the French batteries that his soldiers gave him the honourable nickname of 'The Salamander'."

But Macaulay also felt constrained to say:

> "Cutts indeed had distinguished himself by his intrepidity. But those who most admired him acknowledged that he had neither the capacity nor the science necessary to a general."

A particular enemy of his, Jonathan Swift, went even further and described him as being "as brave and brainless as his sword".

Later on, in 1695, there was an "election" in the Island to choose a Member of Parliament to represent Newport, and the gentlemen of the Island proudly chose their Governor, but Cutts preferred to represent his native Cambridge which had also returned him. Perhaps he rejected the Island's offer ungraciously, and this may have been the beginning of the bad feeling that built up between him and the gentry, and that ultimately led to the Friendship Agreement which was drawn up in 1696.

John, Lord Cutts. As brave and brainless as his sword.

In 1698 he was again in the news when a disastrous fire threatened to burn down the Banqueting House in the Palace of Whitehall. This building had been designed by Inigo Jones, and it was said at the time of the fire that had it not been for the coolness of Lord Cutts, who happened to be there and who organised the Guards to fight the flames, it would most certainly have been destroyed.

Cutts did represent Newport in the first two Parliaments of Queen Anne's reign, but most of his time was spent fighting. He served with great courage and distinction at the battle of Blenheim in 1704 – one of the great decisive battles of the world, as it broke the tremendous power of the French under Louis XIV.

Following this campaign Cutts was appointed Commander-in-Chief in Ireland, a position given to him, so it was said, to keep him out of trouble, for it was appreciated that he was a born fighter and would sooner or later be killed fighting unless he could be protected. If this was the reason for his appointment it had the reverse effect, for it is said to have broken his heart, and he died in Dublin on 26th January 1707, his title dying with him.

Two further comments on the character of this interesting and unusual man are worth noting. One is from a (lady) writer who described him as having had –

> ". . . a sparkling genius, much of humour, and who loved the Muses, and was a good soldier."

The other came from the Reverend E. Boucher James, one time Vicar of Carisbrooke.

> "'The Salamander' was personally as brave an officer as ever headed British troops, and with a small store of Marlborough's calm courage in the midst of tumult, and serenity in danger, he might have had his name inserted in the muster roll of England's famous soldiers."

Henry Wriotheseley, 3rd Earl of Southampton, as a young and gay courtier.

HENRY WRIOTHESLEY
3RD EARL OF SOUTHAMPTON

THE Wriothesley family lived either at Place House, Titchfield, or at Palace House, Beaulieu, both of which had been converted into luxurious private houses from monasteries suppressed in 1536, and given to Thomas Wriothesley, the first Earl of Southampton, for the active part he had played in suppressing them. Thomas Wriothesley became the Lord Chancellor and a very rich man, and in due course his wealth devolved on his grandson Henry Wriothesley, the third Earl, who was in many ways the most interesting member of the family, and the one most closely connected with the Isle of Wight.

He was the second son of his father and was born at Cowdray House, near Midhurst, on 6th October 1573. His father died a few days before his eighth birthday and as his elder brother was already dead, Henry succeeded to the title. At twelve years of age he entered St John's College, Cambridge, and graduated four years later with a Master's degree.

At seventeen he was presented at Court and came to the notice of Queen Elizabeth, and two years later in 1592 when he was nineteen was regarded as the most handsome and accomplished of all the young lords that clustered round the throne. There is no doubt that he was extremely good-looking, and perhaps slightly effeminate with blue eyes and long shoulder-length auburn hair, of which he was very proud. At this time literature became his principal interest and he was on intimate terms with a number of the poets of the day, several of whom dedicated poems to him. As he was of a generous nature and was very rich, he was naturally popular and had many friends in the literary world.

His principal friend was William Shakespeare, who was eight years older, and who in 1593, when Southampton was twenty, dedicated to him his great love poem "Venus and Adonis". The written dedication was fairly formal, but a year later when Shakespeare dedicated to him his other great love poem, "The Rape of Lucrece", the dedication showed that the intimacy between the two men had become very close. Shakespeare also dedicated to him the Sonnets, many of which are erotic in nature and refer to the jealously felt by the author at the relationship between his patron and other poets.

It was at about this time that Southampton gave Shakespeare £1,000, a very large sum of money, to complete a purchase that the poet wished to make.

In 1595 Southampton was twenty-two, unmarried, and extremely eligible on account of his personality and wealth, and he became involved with Elizabeth Vernon, one of the Queen's Ladies-in-Waiting. She was of good family, the daughter of John Vernon of Hodnet, in Shropshire, who was a cousin of the Earl of Essex, but the affair was not regarded with any favour by the Queen, and was adjudged to be injurious to Southampton's reputation. The criticism that this attracted may have influenced him to leave the Court and accompany the Earl of Essex on a military and naval expedition to Cadiz, and when this trip was completed he went on a second and similar voyage to the Azores.

Back at Court in 1598 he became involved one night in a squabble when playing primero (a card game fashionable at the time) with Sir Walter Raleigh and another courtier. They were playing in the Presence Chamber, and were asked to stop by Ambrose Willoughby, one of the Queen's Gentlemen of the Bedchamber, as the Queen was about to go to bed. An argument ensued, Southampton hit Willoughby, and in the scuffle that followed Willoughby pulled out some of Southampton's auburn locks. The following morning the Queen, who had not forgiven Southampton over the Elizabeth Vernon business, complimented Willoughby on his action.

Southampton felt it expedient to leave the Court again, and went with Sir Robert Cecil on a diplomatic mission to Paris. While he was there he received news that Elizabeth Vernon was about to become a mother, and to his credit he immediately returned to London and surreptitiously married her. When the Queen heard of this, as she inevitably did, she was furious, banished them both from Court, and in fact they both served short prison sentences.

Banishment from Court was a bad thing for Southampton, for he went off to Ireland with the Earl of Essex, and became involved in the plot to dethrone the Queen that Essex was hatching. A rising was planned to take place in London on Sunday 8th February 1600, and the night before, Southampton bribed the Players at the Globe Theatre to revive Shakespeare's play "Richard II", as Essex and he believed that this demonstrated how easy it was to dethrone a sovereign. The rising was a complete and rather pathetic fiasco, and both Essex and Southampton were arrested and sent to the Tower.

At their trial they were found guilty, stripped of their titles, and condemned to death. Essex was in fact executed on 25th February, but Sir Robert Cecil pleaded with the Queen for Southampton, and his sentence was commuted to life imprisonment. For the next two years he languished in the Tower, which gave him plenty of time to reflect on the foolish things he had done, and there is no doubt this taught him a lesson.

In the early months of 1603 fortune smiled on him again, for the Queen died and James VI of Scotland came to the throne as James I of England. Now, James had reason to be grateful to Southampton for a service the latter had performed a few years previously which resulted in the failure of a plot to kill the King. Also, James had been a sworn ally of the late Earl of Essex, and he remembered the debt he owed to these two. On his Royal Progress from Scotland to London he sent messengers ahead demanding that Southampton should be released from prison and should meet him in York.

The rest of the third earl's story reads like a fairy-tale. King James heaped honours on him, re-creating him Earl of Southampton, and making him a Knight of the Garter. In July the King visited him at his house in Beaulieu Abbey, and appointed him, for life, as Captain of the Isle of Wight and Carisbrooke Castle, and steward, surveyor, receiver, and bailiff of the royal manors in the Island. All the Isle of Wight gentry visited Beaulieu at this time to do honour to their new Governor.

For the next 20 years the Earl spent much of his time in the Isle of Wight, grateful for the up-turn in his fortunes, and determined not to get into trouble again. He lived not in Carisbrooke Castle, his official residence, which he found cold and unfriendly, but in the secluded little manor of Great East Standen, which was only a few miles away in the centre of the Island. Here he built a bowling green on St George's Down above the house, and every Tuesday and Thursday invited the Island gentry to play bowls with him or, if wet, to play cards. No doubt this generosity contributed greatly to his popularity.

One intriguing thought remains. Did William Shakespeare ever visit him in the Island? There does not appear to be any direct evidence, but in those days the Isle of Wight was possibly even more beautiful and peaceful than it is today, and some of the lines Shakespeare subsequently wrote, such as "This precious stone, set in a silver sea" could well have been suggested to him in the Island, particularly if he had visited the bowling green on St George's Down from which there was a spectacular panoramic view of the sea, both to the north and the south.

Shakespeare almost certainly visited the Earl at Titchfield, where he is believed to have taken his Players and entertained his patron, and it has even been suggested that in the earl's love affair with Elizabeth Vernon, Shakespeare found his plot for "Romeo and Juliet". It is also known that after he had been reinstated by James I the third earl entertained the Queen at Southampton House in London with a performance of "Love's Labour's Lost" given by the Globe Players which included Burbage and Shakespeare.

Henry Wriothesley obviously tired of his Arcadian existence in the Isle of Wight, for in 1624 he sailed for Holland at the head of a contingent of English soldiers, and this proved to be his undoing, for soon after his arrival in the Low Countries he caught a fever and within a few days he was dead.

So ended the career of a most colourful character and a very popular Governor of the Isle of Wight. No-one mourned his passing more than the gentry of the Island who were thus deprived of their Tuesday and Thursday outings to St George's Down and had to find some other way of occupying their time.

H. W. (RAICH) DOE

RAICH DOE was born in Yarmouth, lived in Yarmouth, and died in Yarmouth. Like his father before him he served the harbour and the community, and for many years before his retirement he was the Clerk to the Harbour Commissioners. His father 'Billy' Doe had been one of Yarmouth's most respected Harbour Masters and is still talked about. His uncle too was a public servant and served the community as the town's postman.

Raich thought the world of his father and inherited from him his love of boats, both large and small. Perhaps the only thing he did not see eye to eye with his father about was the choice of his baptismal name. He did not like the name Horatio, and regarded it not as something to live up to, but something to live down. This may be why he was always known as Raich, both in Yarmouth and throughout the Island, and possibly in other parts of the world which he visited in his career as a sailor.

And this name suited him. It was a "one-off", it was individualistic, it had a slightly off-beat ring to it, it had character. It was also warm and friendly. And this really describes the man himself, for he was all of these things, and when you became his friend you knew you had a friend for life.

The other characteristic that Raich Doe possessed was a sense of humour, and this too was individualistic, and slightly quirky. He not only had a sense of humour, but also a sense of the humorous which is not quite the same thing.

Raich was a good raconteur and had a long repertoire of favourite stories about local people. Many of these concerned contemporaries who worked in the harbour, and this is not in the least surprising for the harbour was at the centre of his life. One tale concerned a very large man of 18 stones whose job was boat maintenance and who was somewhat accident prone. This man one day went out to a boat that was leaking badly, to pump the boat out. This he did, and pumped it all into his dinghy that he had tied up alongside. The dinghy promptly sank, and when he came to go ashore he was stuck as he could not reach the dinghy due to the yacht's high topsides. His cries for help were not heard and he was only rescued at midnight when his wife phoned to say her husband had not been home, which was unusual, and – which was much more sinister – he had not been seen in the Wheatsheaf all evening.

'Raich' Doe, Yarmouth's most colourful character.

The same man was working on the engine of a boat one day and dropped a spanner in the bilge. Owing to his girth he found it difficult to reach, so in order to get the maximum length of his arm he lay down on his back and reached down. While in this position the half belt on the back of his boiler suit got hooked round the starting handle, and he was caught. Wriggle as he would he could not get free; he tried to get out of his overalls without success, and it was quite by chance that someone rowing across the harbour several hours later heard him shouting.

A final harbour story concerned another respected engineer who went out to a boat to attend to the engine. Unfortunately his dinghy painter got caught round the propeller and once he started the engine the turning of the shaft gradually wound the dinghy down until its bow was hard up against the A-bracket, and only the transom was showing above water. He too had to be rescued.

As a boy, Raich used to earn a few coppers in his spare time by doing odd jobs. One of these was peeling and chipping potatoes in the local fish and chip shop. The work was hard and not frightfully well paid, but there were compensations and remunerative opportunities. The lady of the house was large and extremely well endowed, and while the potato peeling was in progress she would strip to the waist in the scullery, soap herself well, and have a vigorous wash.

To a schoolboy this was something of an eye opener, and Raich was envied by his friends. So that though the pay was not good he found it possible, and indeed easy, to sub-contract the work for a very satisfactory figure. Hence the experience was of commercial as well as educational value.

Another job was pumping the organ in the Methodist Church. Hymns were sung vigorously, being led by the organist, a lady who on weekdays ran the local butcher's shop. Her voice was noted more for its power than for its accuracy, and he particularly remembered her singing "Jesu, lover of my soul. Let me to thy bosom fly" and idly wondering whether a bosom fly was anything like a horse fly. He had already learned that there were no flies on the fish and chip lady.

Raich Doe was brought up in the Methodist faith, and though he did not become an ardent churchgoer, in later years his views on religion were eminently sensible and thoughtful. On the subject of dwindling church congregations, which is one that exercises the thoughts and minds of many people nowadays, he believed two things. Firstly, that churches should be happy places, and church services happy events, so that people of all ages looked forward to them and found them more attractive than television programmes or pubs. Secondly, Raich believed that the urge to go to church to worship should be fostered at all ages, and that society was neglecting to do this, particularly for teenagers, many of whom quickly lost any good habits they had picked up in their early years.

After leaving Yarmouth School, Raich's education continued at Newport Grammar School. Here they had school on Saturday mornings, which was hard in the summer for any boy with a boat. And on Saturday afternoons he and a few of his cronies used to help an old man in Yarmouth. This was "Sailor" Mann, who had spent all his life in the Navy, and now in his retirement was earning a few bob by delivering luggage from Yarmouth Ferry and Railway Station to the big houses and hotels in the West Wight. Totland was at the height of its popularity at this time, with many large houses and hotels, and there was considerable holiday traffic at the week-ends.

In the playground at the old Grammar School was a single small apple tree, which was the pride and joy of the headmaster. One might say that of all the unfortunate things to have in the playground at a boys' school a lone apple tree must rank high. Inevitably each year the apples disappeared, and equally inevitably there was an enquiry, in fact it ultimately became almost an obsession with the headmaster to preserve his apples.

One year he was so incensed at the disappearance of apples that he kept the whole school in one Saturday afternoon until the culprits confessed, and of course on this particular afternoon the Yarmouth boys were not able to help Sailor Mann hump his usual Saturday quota of heavy cabin trunks, many of which had to be carried from the van and up several flights of stairs. When he finally got home from school, Raich went to see Sailor Mann to apologise, and told him the reason why they had been missing. And that was that.

The next day Sailor contacted him and asked him whether he could rake up one or two friends to help him with a little job he had to do that evening, and Raich was only too happy to oblige, as working with Sailor was always interesting, and profitable.

In the evening they piled into Sailor's van and set off in the direction of Newport. In those days Newport was not the busy town it is today, and on Sunday evening there was no-one at all about. By the time they got there it was quite dark, and Sailor parked his van outside the wall of the Grammar School and climbed over. They all followed him and with fascination watched as he quickly and skilfully attacked the apple tree with a saw and cut it off about a foot from the ground. It was not a very large tree, and between them they managed to carry it across the playground and roll it over the wall and on to the van. Off they set for Yarmouth, only diverting slightly on the way to ditch the tree where it was not likely to be found.

On Monday morning the balloon went up. The headmaster was frantic, the police were called in, and for some days the young culprits lived in fear and trembling, but the perpetrators of the crime were never discovered.

Life in Yarmouth for a young boy was always interesting, for where there are boats there is usually action. On one occasion Raich dived into the harbour and rescued a girl who had fallen in the water and could not swim. He undoubtedly saved her life and was rewarded by her wealthy father with no less than half a crown.

At that time anyone who found a dead body floating in the water was given five shillings, and Raich wryly commented that in fact the girl would have been worth twice as much to him if he had let her drown.

The *Ocean Breeze* story is a strange one and worthy of repeating. In 1940, as a young man of eighteen or nineteen, Raich was serving in a high speed coastal craft belonging to the army. One day he happened to see an advertisement for volunteers to take the Lowestoft steam drifter *Ocean Breeze* down to North Africa. He applied and discovered that the ship, which had been working as a mine sweeper in the North Sea, was to be used as an ammunition support vessel in the forthcoming second front operations. This sounded interesting and exciting, and within forty-eight hours he had travelled to Lowestoft and was at sea.

The voyage took three weeks, as they steamed west out into the Atlantic for four days before turning south, but they arrived safely. The trip was not a pleasant one. As a coal burner with maximum bunker capacity for four days at sea, every available space was filled with coal. The fish hold was full and bags were stacked on deck. As the bunkers emptied so they were refilled from the bags on deck, and the empty bags were then refilled from the loose coal in the fish hold. In heavy weather this must have been quite a task.

Once in North Africa they were kept busy ferrying arms and ammunition along the coast. They took part in the Oran landings, and at dead of night supplied arms to bands of what Raich described as bandits – each man wearing crossed bandoleers, with knives, grenades, etc, at the belt. The attraction of *Ocean Breeze* for this operation was the silence of her steam engine as compared with a diesel. The tale of her exploits in this theatre of war is really another story.

Forty years later Raich was attending a meeting of the Isle of Wight Camera Club, of which he was a member. The speaker on this occasion was a professional photographer who had brought with him a selection of his work. (According to Raich he specialised in ships and nudes.) One of the pictures he was exhibiting was a very fine shot of *Ocean Breeze* rising to a sea with the spray blowing across her bow, this having been taken from Lowestoft pierhead as she left the port for the last time. Raich asked if he could buy the print and the photographer refused, but said he would make a copy. They discussed ways and means of getting this print from Lowestoft to the Isle of Wight without damage, and in the end Raich said that, as he would shortly be attending a caravan rally at Burleigh House near Stamford, he would call and collect it.

In due course the Rally took place, and when it was over Raich went to ring the photographer to check that the picture was ready and that the arrangement for collecting it still held good. There were four temporary telephone booths erected under some trees, with a long queue to each one. It was pouring with rain.

When his turn came he got through to the photographer and asked him if the print of *Ocean Breeze* was ready. He was told that it was, and arranged to pick it up next day. As he finished his call the next man in the queue said: "Excuse me, I could not help hearing you mention *Ocean Breeze*. I served in her during the war when she was a mine sweeper, but we had to leave her in Lowestoft on the day that a new crew were arriving to take her down to North Africa."

This world of ours is indeed a small one.

After the war Raich returned to Yarmouth and picked up the threads of his life again. From an early age he had taken a keen interest in the Boy Scout Movement, and he came to play a leading part in its organisation in the West Wight. He also became a Town Councillor and a member of the Town Trust, the body set up to look after and administer the Town's assets. Indeed he became the Chairman of this body. His love of Yarmouth and of ships shone through everything he did, and for several years he was the energetic Chairman of the Yarmouth Society, promoting the interests of the town and its colourful history.

As Clerk to the Harbour Commissioners he had had an office at the root end of the pier with large picture windows overlooking the Solent. At the top of spring tides the water actually flowed under his office and he seemed to be almost surrounded by it. On the wall was the framed picture of *Ocean Breeze* rising to a sea as she left Lowestoft Harbour on her dangerous voyage.

And somehow this seemed most appropriate. For a sailor to come home from the sea, to take on the responsibility of running his favourite harbour, and to have an office almost surrounded by the incoming tide, cannot be too bad a way to spend a few years, and Raich fitted into his surroundings perfectly.

It was a sad day for many of us when he died, but such is the force of his personality that he will not be forgotten.